# Top Ten Things about the Trucking Industry that You Don't Know...

# And Why it's Costing You Money

Randi L. Paris, LCSW
President & CEO of Ben Freight Trucking, Inc.

## Top Ten Things About The Trucking Industry

# Top Ten Things About The Trucking Industry

Copyright © 2013 by Randi L. Paris

All rights reserved. No part of this book may be used or reproduced in any manner whatsoever without prior written consent of the author, except as provided by the United States of America copyright law.

ISBN-13: 978-0991147809

ISBN-10: 0991147804

DISCLAIMER AND/OR LEGAL NOTICES

The information presented herein represents the view of the author. The author reserves the right to alter and update her opinion based on new conditions. The information presented in the book is based on real life examples showing how you are losing money in the trucking industry. While reading this book, it may evoke emotion in you that may frustrate you or make you angry. If this occurs, please keep an open mind. This book is intended to improve the trucking industry, not exploit it.

# Contents

Dedication .................................................................... vii

Acknowledgements ....................................................... ix

Introduction ................................................................... xi

1  Everyone lies (almost everyone) ................................. 1

2  We need to talk ......................................................... 11

3  Are we even close .................................................... 19

4  Who needs teamwork ............................................... 27

5  I already know .......................................................... 35

6  Spy glasses (a look inside) ....................................... 43

7  Wasting time ............................................................. 55

8  Broken into pieces ................................................... 63

9  He did what, She said what, Who all knows ............ 71

10  How late are you .................................................... 81

    Appendix: Trucker Talk Defined ............................ 93

### Top Ten Things About The Trucking Industry

# Dedication

To my aunt, Nancy Turner, for playing an intricate role in removing stereotypes for me in the trucking industry.

To my father-in-law, Garold Paris, for your dedication to the trucking industry. May I carry on your legacy with the same passion, commitment, and integrity.

To my parents, John and Cheryl Turner, for instilling core values.

Most importantly, to my husband, Ben Paris. We make a great team! Thank you for listening to my vision, giving input for this book, and empowering me to have a voice. Your support is inspiring.

# Top Ten Things About The Trucking Industry

# Acknowledgements

I want to thank everyone involved in creating this book. What a ride it has been!

Ben, my husband, my best friend and business partner.

Nickole Huffman for all of her hard work as the editor of this book. I am so proud of our collaboration. You are talented, humble, and generous.

Melodi Ingalls for your support and advice along this path of becoming an author.

Amber Motz for encompassing what a best friend is and playing a powerful role in my life.

Nicole Gebhardt for providing guidance and support while writing this book.

Rob Root for the encouragement to write a book and own my expertise.

Jessica Laymon, Michele Michalski, and Brandy Sons, for sharing a special bond and showing unconditional support.

My parents for your unconditional love and being a positive influence in my life.

Conlee, Collins, and Mason: I love you and you make me very proud.

# Introduction

I grew up in a small town in Indiana. My mom was a Social Worker and my dad worked in Logistics for a large manufacturing company. As a kid, I was always interested in both of my parents' careers, oftentimes, participating in their work discussions. When I decided to attend graduate school, I chose to get my Masters in Social Work because I wanted to help people, but more importantly, I wanted to understand human behavior. While attending graduate school, I worked full time and lived with my aunt (over the road truck driver for nearly 20 years). My aunt was typically gone for weeks at a time. I fondly remember her coming home and I was excited to hear about her "trucking stories." I found myself fascinated by the industry, the same way I was when I was younger. My aunt Nancy and I would stay up late processing her trucking excursions. We would celebrate her positive encounters in the industry and troubleshoot any negative encounters she experienced by using my social work skill set I was learning in school. I was excited because I realized at that moment, I was learning an invaluable skill through my education that could be transferred into any industry.

My love of the trucking industry continued when I met my husband, Ben, an over the road driver. Soon after I met him, he obtained a local driving job. My father-in-law was also a truck driver for 42 years. The "trucking theme" continued to have dominance in my life, so I decided to leave my career in social work to pursue my love and passion for the trucking industry. Of course, people who knew me could not understand why or how I could switch from social work to trucking, but after understanding my experience and knowledge related to the trucking industry, everyone acknowledged it would be a perfect fit.

Ben Freight Trucking, Inc. was established in January 2012, as a result of wanting to operate a trucking company based on integrity, transparency, and on-time deliveries while treating every individual along the way with dignity. In the first month of operation, it was discovered that the aforementioned reasons for wanting to start a business were needed in the trucking industry.

Ben Freight Trucking is currently building a reputation in the industry by displaying the company's principals through each business transaction. Overall, our experiences in the trucking industry have been positive. We are proud to be working in an important industry. Building solid relationships with companies is part of our mission to providing a great service. Although the majority of our encounters in the trucking industry have been positive, we are recognizing the components that are causing you to *lose* money.

I decided to write this book to offer insight for the trucking industry. This book will highlight the information truck drivers know from being inside the trucking world on a daily basis and why knowing this information can benefit every component of the trucking industry. Some of the information that you read will sound like common sense. The need for implementation of the top ten things this book will focus on will improve the overall functioning of the trucking industry. If a person only implements one of the top ten things this book offers, it will still be beneficial for you as an individual in this industry and for your company.

It is not unusual for truck drivers to talk to everyone they see throughout the day and for the most part, people tend to listen. If you pay close attention to what they are saying, through all of their dirty, funny stories, they truly notice what is happening "inside" the industry. At times the trucker stereotype may keep company personnel from realizing that when they confide in truck drivers, those drivers are in fact listening. Truck drivers pay close attention to what people are saying, especially gossip, and love to share that information with whomever will listen.

I believe everyone in the trucking industry has the same goal: work together to make on-time deliveries with no damaged freight while making money. It sounds easy, but at times, when all components are not working well independently, it can be disastrous. These *Top Ten Things About The Trucking Industry That You Don't Know And Why It's Costing You Money* are instrumental to fostering growth in the trucking industry. No one wants to *lose* money in business, so pay close attention and see what area or areas you can improve on to ensure that you no longer *lose* money.

In the trucking industry there are four components: shipping, brokers, transporters (drivers), and receiving (consignee). Each of the these components work independently to achieve the goal: on-time deliveries with no damaged freight. For clarification, one load of freight being hauled is one transaction in the trucking industry. I break down each chapter with an example to show how you are *losing* money. I understand no one is perfect and there will be human error that will cause malfunctions at some point in this industry. By illustrating the examples in each chapter, it helps you to see how each of these ten things are actually making you *lose* money. The examples used in each chapter are based on real life examples that have either happened to us directly or to someone we know working in the industry. They may sound extreme or exaggerated, but they *are* real examples.

When looking at the overall trucking industry, I feel it is important to understand how important this industry is to our nation's existence. According to American Trucking Association ( ATA) 2011 and 2012 statistics report on Truckinginfo.com:

- In 2011, United States economy depends on trucks to deliver nearly 80 percent of all freight transported annually in the U.S., accounting for $603.9 billion worth of manufactured and retail goods transported by truck in the U.S.
- The trucking companies, warehouses and private sector in the U.S. employs an estimated 8.7 million people in trucking-related jobs; nearly 3.5 million were truck drivers

- Approximately one of every 15 workers in the U.S is employed in the trucking industry
- Estimates of 15.5 million trucks operate in the U.S; approximately 2 million are tractor trailer
- It is an estimated over 3.5 million truck drivers in the U.S; one in nine are independent, a majority of which are owner operators
- It should be noted that out of the 3.5 million truck drivers in the US, women truck drivers account for around 5 percent and minorities account for an estimated 32.6 percent
- **Estimates of 1.2 million trucking companies in the U.S; 97% operate 20 or fewer trucks while 90% operate 6 or fewer trucks**

According to U.S Bureau of Labor Statistics, job growth for tractor-trailer drivers and heavy truck drivers is estimated to increase by 21 percent by 2020. The Department of Labor is projecting a growth in logistics jobs for the next several years and truck drivers will account for approximately 43 percent of those jobs. There is also a projected truck driver shortage (*"Occupational Outlook Handbook, 2012-13"*).

By looking at these statistics, it reaffirms the importance of our industry and that people really do depend on us. We *must* do our part in representing this industry in a respectful manner. I feel there are positive, good people working in this industry. Unfortunately, the negative people and negative situations tarnish the reputation for this industry. I want people to have positive thoughts when hearing "trucking" or anything related to the "trucking industry."

**Top Ten Things About The Trucking Industry**

# Chapter 1

# Everyone lies
(almost everyone)

Yes, honesty is really a chapter in this book. I actually find it to be the *most* important reason why you are *losing* money in the trucking industry and damaging your reputation at the same time. There are four components to the trucking industry: shipper, broker, transporter (drivers), and receiver. Each component works independently, only allowing certain information to be released to the other components on a need to know basis. Sound confusing? It is very confusing!

Each component has an important role in the big picture: making the on-time delivery with no damaged freight with all components making money. If something goes wrong in one of those components, it will affect the final outcome; therefore, costing *everyone* in the trucking industry money. I will break this down further in each chapter. For this chapter, honesty is the starting point for all parties involved in order to achieve one successful transaction.

If dishonesty occurs at any point throughout the transaction, there is a greater chance for error or the inability to forgive an error. In trucking, the more forthright with information you are, the more respected you are as an individual. This is the reputation that you want in the industry; not one who lies or stretches the truth in fear of losing business. Let's look at an example in each component of the trucking industry to see how dishonesty is making you *lose* money.

## Shipping

When the broker and carrier are on the same page and conducting business honestly, it is still imperative for the shipping component to use the same honesty policy. Shipping sets the tone for the entire transaction. For example, if a driver pulls into the place of business to pick up the load, she may meet dishonest staff members who simply do not want to load her quickly. They make excuses such as, "I have to take my lunch, so we will have to load you in a few minutes," (which could potentially mean hours) or "There are several trucks in front of you waiting to be loaded," (giving no time frame). This happens *more* than it should in the industry.

I am perplexed by this as a trucking company owner because the shipping component is the company who *is* usually the actual paying customer or shipping the freight to the receiving company (who is the paying customer). What? Yes, the company who is shipping the freight pays the freight broker to broker the load to a carrier or pays the carrier directly. So, why would there ever be problems from the shipping and receiving components that would *cost* everyone more money, especially their own company? After a driver waits to load for more than two hours, a detention fee can be added to the original rate. The detention fee varies from company to company. Also, the shipper has to pay employees overtime if they have to stay later to load a truck, hence *costing* their own company to *lose* even more money.

Here is the big reason this dishonesty is *costing* you money: the executives from the companies may not be aware of the dishonesty from their employees. The shipping staff tell their superiors the delay in loading the truck is due to broker or driver error. Do you think all employees are going to be honest with their superiors regarding their lack of effort to load freight? If the employees were staying on task and doing their jobs according to protocol, there would be no need for dishonesty on the part of the shipping component. Another reason may be that the employees at the shipping company may not feel comfortable discussing problems with the supervisor, if something were to go wrong by accident.

## Brokers

When a company is shipping freight, they either choose a carrier directly or use a freight broker. For this example, let's say the company chooses to use a freight broker and negotiates a certain rate with the broker agreeing to find a carrier (trucking company or owner-operator) to transport the freight to make an on-time delivery. This is where dishonesty can hurt you and make you *lose* money.

Sometimes brokers know they are not able to find a carrier to meet the time sensitive deadlines, but they still agree to broker the load for fear of potentially losing that customer. When this happens, it forces them into "panic mode" as they desperately try to find a willing driver to haul the freight and sometimes they are limited on the quality of drivers or trucking companies. The freight brokers have to always be cognizant of not *losing* money on the load, so they are also looking for a carrier to haul the freight for a low rate. See the predicament? This becomes a snowball effect. The broker selects a driver because they "say" they can meet the deadline for delivery for the low rate.

## Transporter (Drivers)

Once the driver who was selected by the freight broker starts out to make the delivery, she realizes there is *no* way she can make that delivery on time. What should she do? Well, what she should do and what she does are not usually the same thing. It is *best* policy for the driver to use honesty with the broker along the way and/or to the company who is receiving the load. Instead, this driver has decided to be dishonest due to the fact that she is afraid of not getting future loads from this freight broker. Does it sound a little backward? People tend to lie out of fear, especially fear of *losing* money and business.

The receiving company calls the broker to see when the driver will arrive with the load. Let's say for the sake of this example, delivery time is 5pm. The broker calls the driver and says, "Will you make the delivery time at 5pm?" Remember, the driver knows she will not be able to meet the 5pm deadline, so instead of admitting that it is not possible for the load to be delivered at the requested time, the response is, "Of course, I will be there at 5pm." When 5pm comes and goes, the receiving company thinks the load is a "no-show." The receiving company is furious and calls the broker and asks, "Where is the load that was promised to be here at 5pm?"Tempers flare and everyone is *mad* at everyone!

The broker calls and calls the driver, however, the driver decides to not take the call and shows up for delivery time at 7pm. Do you think the receiving company is happy to see the driver and receive the freight? No. Actually, the receiving team at the company went home and the driver is unable to deliver the load. Now, the driver is stuck overnight with the load and no one knows at this point when she will be able to unload it. Who *loses* money in this situation? *Every* component *loses* money, as well as credibility in the industry, all because of choosing to be dishonest.

## Receiving

The receiving company is the last part of the transaction. This is the company that ordered the freight for it to be shipped. It is possible that the receiving company may be the paying customer instead of the shipping company. Either way, shipping and receiving components are similar: they load and unload the freight that is being hauled and pay for the freight. Sometimes receiving companies have the same issues as the shipping company. There could be a list of things that could go right when receiving freight or a list of things that could go wrong. Honesty plays a huge role in *why* companies are *losing* money.

When a driver pulls into the facility for an on-time delivery, a person may think, "I wonder what could happen when a delivery arrives on time?" Well, a few things could go wrong. The guard shack employee may abuse his power and lie to the driver, telling her she *must* wait. Or, he may allow a truck that arrived after you to push ahead of you in line and get unloaded first, causing confusion and chaos. And, some employees may not want to exert the energy to unload the truck. Laziness settles in and motivation goes out. So, what happens?

The driver waits, gets frustrated, and may even lose her temper and cause a scene. If you were an outsider looking in on this situation, it looks like the driver is being rude and unprofessional for no apparent reason. However, in this example, who pays the price? Remember, any wait time over two hours could potentially turn into detention fees incurred by the receiving company. With that being said, do you think the superiors or owners of the receiving company realize their employees are making obstacles that *cost* their own company money? Do the owners of the company keep track of all of the times they had to pay extra fees for not getting the job done on time? These are all questions that need to be asked in order to rectify why companies are *losing* money. Truck drivers see first-hand what is going on "inside" your company on a daily basis.

## Lesson Learned

In order for the beginning of the transaction to start off right, the shipping employees *must* be honest with themselves and their superiors. Sometimes they are overworked and they are doing the best they can; yet sometimes there are those who are being dishonest with everyone involved and unfortunately, it ultimately affects the shipping and receiving companies. If drivers experiences rude, unprofessional behavior or dishonesty from a shipping or receiving company, do you think they will want to take freight from that company again? No, quite honestly, it puts a bad taste in the mouth of truck drivers. And guess what? Truck drivers talk to their peers and let them know the intricacies of what they have to go through when dealing with a company that ships or receives freight.

The shipping and receiving companies need to do random quality checks with brokers, truck drivers, and customers to see if there are any issues they can resolve to enhance the flow of the transaction and to not *lose* money.

In this example, dishonesty on the part of the broker from the initial agreement with the shipping company led to finding a driver in a panic for a low rate, which snowballed into more dishonesty from the driver not being able to deliver the load on time. The desired outcome was not achieved due to each component choosing to be dishonest with themselves and each other. This example happens at an alarming rate in the trucking industry. A person might initially *lose* business if they are honest about time restrictions with delivery and their inability to deliver within the requested time frame but the risk of *losing* money is far greater for all components involved, not to mention the risk of damaging your reputation if you promise an outcome you simply cannot deliver.

## Malfunctions

There are situations that may arise, such as maintenance malfunctions that may prevent you from making the on-time delivery. If a driver has awareness on his or her skill level and are honest with his or her ability to make the timely delivery, it is easier to be honest with the broker as soon as a tire blows out or any other equipment failure. Once a driver communicates the malfunction with the broker, the broker is able to communicate the situation with the other components in the equation making it easier for all parties to problem-solve collaboratively.

People in this industry know equipment malfunctions are inevitable from time to time, but as long as people do not malfunction in their honesty, collaboration will be easy and effective. If the receiving company understands the status of a malfunction they are more likely to extend their hours of operation to receive the freight later in the night, as opposed to thinking the driver is absent or a no-show. Again, this is an example of where honesty can save you money, future business, and your reputation as an individual and the company you represent.

## Important Reminders

- Be honest from the beginning of transaction (all components)
- When you are fearful, be honest
- Lies will create more lies (snowball effect)
- Be honest about your skill level (if you can make the on-time delivery, or if you are not able to find a reputable carrier)
- Shipping and receiving companies need to do quality checks to ensure their employees are not *costing* them more money by delaying load and unload time
- Be honest when you have malfunctions or you need help
- Do not be afraid to do quality checks with all components
- Choosing to not be aware of the problems in your own component is the same as being dishonest

- Avoiding communication (i.e. phone calls, emails, texts) is a form of dishonesty
- Dishonesty tarnishes reputation

**Top Ten Things About The Trucking Industry**

## Chapter 2

# We need to talk?...

How can something so simple as communication be so complex? Communication tends to give a lot of people trouble. Why? Maybe people are not in tune with how they feel or understand the importance of communication. Maybe people are afraid to hurt someone's feelings or letting someone down. Maybe people don't want to admit they are over-committed or poor managers. For whatever reason, communication is the key to success in any relationship, especially business. With all of the on-the-go technology today, it is virtually impossible not to be a successful communicator. Sadly, there is still a lack of communication, especially in the trucking industry.

I feel that communication is the basis of any personal relationship, so it is a "no-brainer" that communication is a value for my trucking company. Honesty and communication, go hand in hand when doing business.

Again, it sounds simplistic saying that communication is a reason why you as a business are *losing* money in the trucking industry. When there is a breakdown in communication there tends to be chaos that follows.

Each component in the trucking industry must work well independently for the outcome of on-time deliveries with no damaged freight to be achieved. And, as stated in the previous chapter, each component shares information on a need to know basis *only*.

This drives me a little crazy! Remember, communication is a part of my main value system personally and professionally, so of course, a lack of transparency is hard to understand. It is also important to communicate in a professional manner: tone, content, and especially language. As a reminder, when using a professional tone, stay calm and do not yell. Also, when you are speaking, make sure you are not accusing, attacking, or complaining. Most importantly, do not cuss or use language or content that would degrade a person. When you are texting or emailing, make sure you are using the same professionalism mentioned above along with being clear and concise. If you communicate in a rude, unprofessional manner, there is a greater chance you will ruin your working relationship. Let's talk about examples of why communication or lack of communication is making you *lose* money in each component.

## Shipping

A shipping company has decided they need to ship freight. A great place to start would either be using a carrier (driver or trucking company) directly or hiring a freight broker to find a carrier. Usually when shipping companies use freight brokers, they tend to use the same ones over and over. The ultimate goal for the shipping company is to get the freight shipped on time and ensure the freight is not damaged to the receiving company.

For this example, the Logistics Coordinator for the shipping company has decided to ship freight using a broker. The Coordinator contacts the broker and explains what type of freight that needs to ship, including other pertinent information that is significant for the negotiation process. Even though the shipping company is entrusting this broker to "take care" of its freight by finding a driver, the communication is limited. The Logistics Coordinator at the shipping company likes to communicate through email only. The freight broker feels he understands the needs of the shipping company from the information in the email. What could go wrong? There is nothing wrong with communicating through email as long as you get all the information and ensure that the information is communicated to all components of the transaction. Did this Logistics Coordinator communicate with the shipping department at his own company? Is the receiving company aware of the freight that will be arriving? Have the date and time been provided? Do you see all of the communication errors that take place and make you *lose* money? Communication is a *must*.

## Brokers

Let's continue the above example: the broker has the information in an email format. The broker is responsible for finding a great carrier to fulfill this order. The broker goes through a list of trustworthy drivers (owner operators) and makes contact with a driver. The driver needs information before agreeing to haul any freight. The broker explains all of the information regarding this load by reading the email sent from the shipping company. The truck driver is confused by the lack of information and asks several questions to the broker. Freight brokers can only guarantee and communicate information they have from the shipping company. Sometimes brokers only want to give limited information to truck drivers for various reasons. These reasons could include a fear of owner-operators working out a deal directly with the logistics company (back door policy), the information from the shipper could be confidential, or the broker withholds information to convince a company or owner-operator to haul low end freight.

The truck driver agrees to take the load based on the information provided by the broker regarding the load. This is where it is extremely easy for dishonesty to creep in and contribute to the breakdown of communication. The broker has *no* idea if the receiving company has been notified to receive this load. He is depending on the information to be accurate and expecting the Logistics Coordinator to communicate all of the details with all components. Can you see the importance of communication? Can you see how a lack of communication can make you *lose* money?

## Transporter (Drivers)

The driver has the rate confirmation from the broker heading to make the on-time delivery. She is confident and excited about this load. The driver feels the broker is impressive with his knowledge and hopes to work with this brokerage again in the future. As the delivery time gets closer, the broker calls the driver to double check that delivery will be timely. The driver ensures the broker it will be there early and asks for the receiving company's contact information to inform them of the arrival time. This might sound like a relatively simple request, however, the broker states, "I will contact them as communication goes through me." What? Why? That is the way communication works the majority of the time in the trucking industry: you are on a need-to-know basis.

The driver arrives at the receiving company. There is no one there to greet her at the guard shack and the lights are off at this location. A little panic sets in with the driver because she has to be somewhere early tomorrow to pick up a load that she is already committed to. What happens when no one is there to receive the load? Who did not communicate? Why was the driver not permitted to contact the receiving company? And, why should this lack of communication *cost* you money?

## Receiving

The receiving company was never notified of the arrival time throughout the duration of this entire transaction from the shipping company or from the broker and, of course, the driver (not allowed to communicate). What happens next? Well, when there is absolutely no communication or there is a breakdown in communication, the first thing that happens is pointing fingers and placing blame. Who is going to pay the most for this communication error?

In this scenario, it is the truck driver because she is stuck with the load and will be unable to pick up her scheduled load for tomorrow morning. This hurts the driver or the trucking company's bottom line. Who *else* pays? Once the receiving company realizes this is not the fault of the driver, it may decide to pay employees overtime to go into work to unload the freight. The receiving company can then invoice the shipping company or brokers for the extended labor. Again, in the trucking industry, when there is an error in one component, it is likely for the outcome to be a mess and *every* component *loses* money.

## Lesson Learned

There are numerous reasons why communication is compartmentalized in the trucking industry. First of all, brokers might be afraid of the "Back Door Policy," which means drivers might work out a deal to cut out the broker (middle man) and work directly with the shipping and receiving companies. When people in business feel threatened, they tend to hold back information that could be shared. Communicating information and resources can *only* empower each component to work as a team. This will result in each component wanting to collaborate in the future.

A necessary tool that will be useful in the trucking industry is for each component to understand what the other components are doing during the transaction. The more knowledge a person has, the more valuable and understanding he or she can be throughout the process. How would the previous example have been different if communication was the number one goal throughout the entire transaction as opposed to secrecy for fear of losing business?

## Malfunctions

There will always be malfunctions that come up when there are four components working independently to solve a puzzle. If communication is transparent throughout the process, it will help all parties work collaboratively to resolve any malfunctions. Communication is key to building relationships, so when a problem arises, as long as there is communication, people tend to stay calm and want to help. It is easier to be "solution-focused" instead of "problem-focused" if communication is the platform.

## Important Reminders

- Communicate all of the information you have regarding the transaction being carried out
- Use email, text, or phone to communicate
- Know when to pick up the phone to communicate in person
- Be mindful of the tone you set when communicating via text or email
- You can never *over* communicate
- It is nice to communicate via email to create a communication log (accountability)
- Create a log of all telephone calls
- Breakdown in communication usually causes chaos
- Communication will make it easier to work with someone
- Effective communication creates a positive working relationship
- Communication helps resolve conflict or potential conflict

- If you communicate in a rude, unprofessional manner, there is a greater chance you will ruin your working relationship
- Try to be succinct in your thoughts when communicating
- It is helpful to be "solution-focused" than "problem-focused" when communicating

## Chapter 3

# I already know...

Lack of knowledge is my third reason I feel you are *losing* money. It is always important to make sure you obtain knowledge in all areas of life, especially in the business you decide to work in or own. In the trucking industry, if you do not have knowledge, you *will* get run over! I talked about the four components working independently on a need-to-know basis with relating information; therefore, if you are not knowledgeable about all aspects of the trucking industry, how do you know what is going on from day to day? How are you able to figure out the information you are not being told? Sound tricky? It is! Having knowledge in your area of expertise along with knowledge in the other areas, puts you at an advantage in this industry.

This industry moves at a fast pace and decisions are made in seconds. If you are not equipped with knowledge, you *lose* money from the beginning of the transaction until the end of it. If this happens on a daily basis, you will be out of business within weeks and you will also lose credibility in the industry.

How do you as a shipper, broker, driver, and receiver obtain the knowledge necessary to not *lose* money?

1. Understand the ins and outs of the component you are working in and become an expert in that component
2. Understand the ins and outs of the *other* components in the trucking industry
3. Be patient and work collaboratively with the other components; trusting relationships will form
4. Make sure there is respectful communication; it is easier to learn and gain knowledge in a positive environment
5. Do not be afraid to ask questions to anyone in the trucking field---knowledge is power!

Remember, the more information you have regarding the industry you work in, the more prepared you will be when operating your end of the transaction. Just think, in a perfect world, you can work with a knowledgeable person from start to finish. What would that experience be like? Would everyone be satisfied and *make* money? I guarantee, no one *loses* money. With that being said, I will show you an example of how a lack of knowledge in the trucking industry can cost you money as a shipper, broker, driver, and receiver.

## Shipping

For this example, the shipping company needs to ship freight out as soon as possible. The Logistics Coordinator is in a frenzy due to having a "hot load" (load that should have already been delivered to the receiving company). The Logistics Coordinator is too busy to find a carrier, so he calls his trusty freight broker. He decides to pick up the phone to discuss this hot load. While the broker is asking the Logistics Coordinator details regarding the freight, he recognizes that the Logistics Coordinator is not fully engaged in the conversation because he is working diligently to put out other fires regarding this shipment. The broker senses the desperation and decides to upcharge the Logistics Coordinator by insisting this load is an emergency and requires an additional fee. Because the Logistics Coordinator is desperate to see the freight delivered, he quickly agrees.

The broker charges the shipper an additional $100 to expedite this load; the same load the shipping company always expedites. The shipping company has already *lost* $100 because it lacked the knowledge regarding usual expedited fees.

## Brokers

The broker that was able to upcharge the shipping company feels great about the extra money he is making for his company. The broker decides he is going to make his company more money by finding a carrier to expedite this load at a cheaper rate. The broker contacts a company that states it can take the load for the cheap rate and will make the on-time delivery. The broker takes pride in the great work of up-charging the shipper and low balling the carrier. So far in this example, the shipper and driver are *losing* money.

## Transporter (Drivers)

The driver gets the rate confirmation and information regarding this load from his dispatcher. He is excited about getting an expedited load. He knows there will be no wait time to back into the dock and freight will be a quick load and unload. When the trucking company negotiated this load with the broker, it failed to realize the road construction en route to this delivery that will put the driver out of route an additional 50 miles, not to mention the toll roads along the way. With the calculations for this load now, it appears the trucking company will *lose* $100 on this load. This loss doesn't even factor in the wear and tear on equipment. At this point, the broker is the only component making money on this transaction.

## Receiving

The driver makes the delivery on time despite all of the rerouting for construction and toll roads. The receiving team is happy to see the driver and welcomes him right into the dock as expected. Remember, this is a hot load that the receiving team *needs* in order to meet the demands of its customers. As the unloading of freight is underway, the receiving company realizes the freight is damaged. What? Does this happen? Yes, it happens when the freight is not loaded properly, there's erratic driving, and when the load is not properly secured. What happens next? In this example, the receiving company refuses the load due to damaged freight.

Each component is placing blame and is furious; especially with the driver. Who *lost* money in this example? All four components lost money! The loss of money is due to a lack of knowledge in their own specialty, and a lack of knowledge by not understanding the other components in their industry.

The shipping company *lost* money from the beginning by not having knowledge and understanding and was taken advantage of by the broker. The trucking company did not have an understanding of the cost structure to operate the truck. And, lastly the receiving team refused the load and lost their customers as a result of the damaged freight. The receiving company will also stop doing business with the shipping company and the shipping company will no longer do business with the broker. And, the broker will not give the trucking company another chance in the future. Do you see how lack of knowledge spiraled out of control and everyone *lost* money and future business?

## Lesson Learned

This example happens more than it should in the trucking industry. One way for you not to *lose* money is to have knowledge in your own area of expertise. It is also beneficial for you to invest time in gaining knowledge for the other areas in your industry that you must depend on to complete a successful transaction. There are many opportunities for conferences, collaboration, and workshops that provide education on each component. You can also go to the one common denominator of each component: Truck Drivers.

Here is an idea for people in the trucking industry: maybe if you want to gain knowledge in either a specific component or all of the components, ask a truck driver. Truck drivers collaborate with all components daily. It is better to ask questions to be better equipped to fix the problems instead of waiting for Ralph the mouthy truck driver to possibly air it out on the CB.

Trust me, anything negative that goes wrong in the trucking industry has the potential to get passed along on the CB or at truck stops. A driver is the one component that deals with the shipper, broker, *and* receiver. With that knowledge, it would benefit drivers to truly understand each component to ensure quality is being achieved. It would also benefit the other components to spend time understanding what it is like for truck drivers in this industry. I believe it would be a great idea for people working in other components to ride along with a truck driver for a week as part of their company's training. It would highly benefit all parties involved and would offer insight on demands, communication (or lack thereof), and the obstacles that a truck driver faces when delivering different types of loads.

Another situation that is possible in this example: the shipping company loads previously damaged freight onto the truck and the driver is unaware because he is not allowed on the dock during loading (due to shipping company's policy). In this situation, the driver needs to mark on the "Bill of Lading" (BOL) with the following code, "SLC," which means, "shipper load and count." This is important for the driver, when not present for the loading, as the implications of transporting a "SLC" are important. Trucking companies are usually liable for the full value of the goods they transport but if they are not present for the loading, they are not responsible for the condition of the freight. Instead, responsibility lies on the shoulders of those who loaded the freight. After the driver pulls out of the dock, he should pull over to a safe place to inspect the freight. If damaged freight is discovered, the driver should take photos of the freight and immediately send them to the broker. He should then return to the dock to discuss the condition of the freight with the shipping supervisor on duty. This will ensure proper communication by channeling through the chains of command and will enable the broker to contact the receiving company to communicate the issue of damaged freight and determine the best way to proceed.

## Malfunctions

Malfunctions to the original plan can be evoked by circumstances out the driver's control, such as construction or accidents, on any route or during any part of the transaction. Being fully prepared before negotiating the deal is the key to a great outcome: on-time delivery without damaged freight and no one *losing* money. Companies need to create a safety plan with proper protocol to ensure the drivers have the knowledge to make well informed decisions in case of malfunctions en route. Understanding the freight you are shipping, brokering, hauling, or receiving is vital to the success of everyone involved in a deal. Also, understanding a potential malfunction is a must in the trucking industry. Problems will arise, let's face it. Vehicles will crash, construction projects will span over miles and miles of the highway, and routes will need to be reconfigured. The more prepared and educated you are, the less stress for your drivers, the more confidence the other components will have for you, and the better your business will be for it!

In the previous example, the freight was damaged and as a result, it was refused. This is not an ideal situation for any of the components involved here. If the goal of each component of the trucking industry is to make on-time deliveries with no damaged freight while making money, the goal was clearly not met here. Because the loading company failed to load the freight properly, all components missed the goal and wasted their time and money. To succeed in the main goal, it is important that we educate ourselves in order to prevent problems. Understanding your cost structure is extremely important to obtaining the goals, as well. You must know about equipment (what they have vs. what is needed), fuel mileage (in case of a rerouting, will the driver have what is needed to fuel the truck?), knowing the location of toll roads en route and on possible reroutes, and the knowledge of how freight will need to be secured, if necessary. It is also important to educate drivers on proper protocol when freight is damaged and how to proceed when it is discovered.

## Important Reminders

- Knowledge is an amazing tool
- Look for experts in your field---don't underestimate truck drivers
- Don't be afraid to ask questions to anyone in order to obtain the necessary information
- Prepare for malfunctions by having a safety plan
- Understand the freight you are shipping, brokering, hauling, or receiving
- Understand your company's cost structure
- Know how to properly secure freight and have necessary equipment available to do so
- Always document any malfunctions during any point of the transaction---no matter how minor
- It is irresponsible to arrive at the receiving company without knowledge that the freight is damaged
- All components should happily share knowledge with one another

**Chapter 4**

# Are we even close?...

Negotiation is vital to the trucking industry. Your ability to negotiate will directly influence how lucrative your business is. So far, I have discussed honesty, communication, and knowledge as three areas you must understand in order to not *lose* money in the trucking industry. All three of these areas contribute to your ability to negotiate. Negotiation is a game of who has the most knowledge on the subject. This is where you *must* know the cost structure of your own company. If you do not know your bottom line, you are in trouble and will *lose* money.

In order to be effective at negotiating in trucking, whether you are the shipper, broker, driver, or receiver, you must have knowledge in logistics if you do not want to *lose* money. When looking at logistics, you need to know the following: labor required by driver, commodity shipped, mileage and time needed, time frames of pickup/delivery, and whether or not the load works in a driver's schedule.

Negotiation happens in the beginning when a broker obtains contract freight directly from a shipper or when a trucking company obtains contract freight directly from a shipper. When freight is brokered through a broker to a carrier, negotiation takes place for each load. Company drivers do not negotiate the loads; only independent carriers and owner-operators have the ability to negotiate their loads. Let's take a look at an example to illustrate why you need to understand how to properly negotiate in order to not *lose* money in all components in this industry.

## Shipping

In this example, the shipper needs to ship freight as soon as possible. The freight needs to be secured, and is almost a full truck load. The Logistics Coordinator contacts the broker by telephone to explain the situation. The Logistics Coordinator fails to understand the *cost* of the freight she needs to ship. She wants to save hauling expenses, so she brokers a low amount to ship the freight. The Logistics Coordinator feels good about the savings for her company by going through this particular broker and negotiating a low rate.

## Brokers

The broker is excited to work with this Logistics Coordinator. This brokerage company has actively pursed this company for a few years. The broker feels that by agreeing to negotiate a low rate, this Logistics Coordinator will always use them in the future. The broker is hoping to upcharge them to make more money on future loads. At this point, the broker is barely covering expenses with the low rate he negotiated. The broker is hoping to find a trucking company that will take an even lower rate. The search for a low rate hauling company begins. The broker calls multiple companies before settling on a trucking company that agrees to ship the freight for a lower rate, making the broker more money. So, at this point in the example, the shipping company and broker are making money. Do you see any problems with these negotiation skills? It looks like everything will work out.

## Transporter (Drivers)

The dispatcher at the trucking company sends the information to one of his drivers with instructions on how to haul this freight. The truck driver is ready to go, especially because the receiving company is in her hometown and the driver will get to visit with her family. It sounds like a win-win situation for everyone involved in this example.

The dispatcher calls the driver and needs her to stop and pick up a few skids along the way for another shipping company. The trucking company makes this cost-effective decision to help offset the loss of the money in accepting the lower rate during negotiation phase. For this example, I will call the extra skids load shipment A, and the secured load shipment B.

The driver stops to make the pick-up for shipment A first, which gets loaded in the front of the truck. This is problematic because it is scheduled to be unloaded first. At this point, the driver should contact her dispatcher to inform him of the situation but instead, she gets annoyed by the extra work and decides after she picks up shipment B, she will not worry about securing the freight.

The first delivery stop is shipment A. Remember, this load is in the front of the truck. It is a disaster. The receiving company refuses the load. They refuse to unload another shipment to receive their freight; therefore, making the shipper, broker, driver, and receiving company *lose* money on shipment A. The driver calls her dispatcher regarding the situation. The dispatcher decides to have the driver deliver shipment B to its destination and return to deliver shipment A. This driver is now backtracking, wasting extra fuel, miles, and time. When the driver pulls in to deliver shipment B, the receiving company refused it because it was not properly secured in the trailer. During the negotiation process with all three components for shipment B, it was mandatory that freight be secured. What happened in this example? This appears to be a situation where irresponsibility and laziness have cost all components money. Was there a lack of understanding or communication during the negotiations? Did the negotiator get caught up in "the right price" and not pay attention to specifics and demands that were being presented during this time?

## Receiving

When the truck pulled into the first receiving company for the shipment A, there was no way a company would unload another company's freight, so it was refused. Everyone *lost* money on that load. Shipment B was refused, too, because the receiving company requested the freight to be secured in order to accept it. Everyone *lost* money on that load, as well. How can each component avoid these mistakes when negotiating? Is paying low rates more important than timely deliveries, damaged freight, and mismanaged goods?

## Malfunctions

Of course, as previously discussed, malfunctions are inevitable in the trucking industry but let me make it clear that not understanding your company's bottom line and logistics during negotiations is NOT a malfunction. You *must* be educated and mentally prepared before entering into any type of negotiation no matter how eager you are to seal the deal. This will enable you to avoid any missing information that is presented as non-negotiable during the negotiation process.

In this example, the Logistics Coordinator did not understand the value of her freight, making it impossible for others to know its value. Because the value of freight was not communicated, the broker wanted to pay the trucking company a lower rate thus resulting in the driver believing that he or she was delivering "cheap freight." The receiving company had no choice but to refuse the load due to the "malfunctions"(or ignorance) of the other components. These malfunctions also prevented the driver from visiting her family and consequently, cost her an extra day on the road.

## Lesson Learned

In this example, it was a "perfect storm" from the beginning of the negotiation to the end. This is what happens when the shipper does not understand logistics. The Logistics Coordinator's only priority was her company's bottom line instead of the freight being shipped. This happens: Sadly, this occurs from time to time in the trucking industry. Each component needs to know that as long as there is "cheap freight," no component will care about it. When freight is not valued by the shipping or receiving company, why should a broker or driver care? Should the paying customers care more about their freight by placing a higher value on it? Understanding the value of the freight is very important during the negotiation phase and each component should be informed of how to make sure it is treated as something of great worth.

When each component is in the negotiation phase, there needs to be a common goal of not pricing freight too low. If this happens, there will be continued malfunctions in all areas, creating a precedent for the trucking industry. This will result in a *loss* of money for every component and will hurt the trucking industry. In the 60's and 70's, freight was respected and shippers and receivers paid higher rates than what is being paid now. It might seem difficult to believe, but it is true. Veteran truck drivers will confirm the rates trucking companies are receiving now as comparable to the rates in the 60's and 70's with fuel being 1/5 of the cost. I find this trend problematic for the trucking industry.

Each component cannot be afraid to *make* money in the negotiation phase. Understand the skills you have as an employee in the trucking industry. Do not be afraid to say the word, "no!" Sometimes the word "no" is quite powerful in negotiation. If you know your skill level, know the variables in the deal, and understand that you get what you pay for, negotiation will be easy.

## Important Reminders

- Understand Logistics when working with any part of the trucking industry

- Shippers and Receivers need to value their freight by considering the importance of their product, so everyone else in the trucking industry will value it
- Shippers and Receivers need to understand what it *costs* to completely transport their freight (beginning to the end)
- It is unfortunate when the shipping company works extremely hard to push out the product and fails to place importance on shipping freight
- Cheap freight is setting a precedent in the trucking industry
- You get what you pay for
- Use honesty, communication, and knowledge when negotiating
- Understand what the fuel surcharge is currently before negotiating
- Do not be afraid to make money when negotiating
- Know your skill level and value before negotiating
- Do not be afraid to say "no" when negotiating
- Understand cost structure associated with each load
- Obtain information regarding the load before you begin to negotiate
- Do not be afraid to ask questions

Chapter 5

# Who needs teamwork?...

Collaboration is not a new concept, but an essential one if you do not want to *lose* money in the trucking industry. The concept of collaboration has been around for years. As a kid, you might have heard "work as a team" or use "teamwork" to get the task or job done. Collaboration must be added to the company's vision for every component in the trucking industry to make money. If you recall, I talked about how each component in the trucking industry must work well independently. With that understanding, it is also imperative for each component to collaborate successfully in order to achieve the desired outcome: on-time deliveries with no damaged freight and every component making money.

In order to be successful in the trucking industry, you must learn to collaborate with the other components. I hear it time and time again how upset everyone gets in this industry when a component refuses to collaborate. To me, collaboration is the answer for every component to make money. Without collaboration, each component fails. Every component needs to collaborate in order for each transaction to go smoothly. I have noticed when collaboration is unsuccessful in the trucking industry, relationships are ruined and are not easily repaired. I have talked about honesty, communication, knowledge, and negotiation thus far in this book. Each and every one of these are essential in understanding how to collaborate in any area of your life; especially in the trucking industry. Let's take a look at an example of where refusing to collaborate in the trucking industry can make you *lose* money.

## Shipping

The shipping company decides they need to ship freight by the end of the week. The Logistics Coordinator calls his favorite, cheap broker to work out the specifics on the load. After talking to the broker, the Logistics Coordinator decides to email all of the information regarding the load to ensure the broker has all of the correct information.

It appears in this example the Logistics Coordinator is doing a great job collaborating with the broker. So, do you think the Logistics Coordinator collaborated with his own shipping department? I talk about the main four components of needing to collaborate, however, I firmly believe that every employee who takes part in a transaction (no matter the role), needs to be informed of all pertinent information to complete the transaction successfully. These employees are an intricate part of the process, thus making it easy to work collectively with all components. Freight does not get loaded or unloaded unless the employees in the shipping and receiving companies are notified.

## Brokers

After communicating with the Logistics Coordinator, the broker is optimistic about working with the shipping company. The broker locates an owner-operator to haul this freight. The broker decides she wants to pay the truck driver a lower rate, knowing the risks involved with this decision. The broker feels confident in her decision with low balling the owner-operator. The truck driver decides to take the cheap freight because it fits into his company's structure. Everyone seems happy at this point and collaboration seems to be going extremely well. How can a lack of collaboration make you *lose* money?

## Transporters (Drivers)

The owner-operator gets the rate confirmation from the broker and heads out to pick up the freight. When the driver arrives to pick up the freight from the shipping company, the driver is informed he is not allowed in the facility unless he is wearing a long sleeve shirt, pants, safety vest, hard hat, ear plugs, and safety glasses. The driver is furious, to say the least, because he is wearing shorts and sandals. The broker did not inform him of the attire requirements in order to pick up this freight.

The owner-operator calls the broker to inform him of this situation. The broker explains to the driver that he will call the shipping company to see if they will work with them on this situation. The broker calls the driver and insists that he purchase the proper attire in order to enter the facility to pick up the freight. The driver realizes he had all of the attire in his truck except a hard hat and safety vest. What should the driver do in this situation? Do you see where the lack of collaboration has led the broker and the driver? Will the delivery be on time now? There are a lot of questions when one or all components fail to work together.

## Receiving

After the truck driver went to a store to purchase the safety vest and hard hat, he was able to pick up the load. On his way to deliver the load, he called the broker to inform him the load would be late due to the delay of not having the proper attire. The broker called the receiving company to inform the supervisor on duty of the situation and reason for the delay. The receiving company advises the broker that receiving will shut down soon, so the driver will have to be there early in the morning to unload the freight. The receiving company understood the dilemma but could not afford to pay employees overtime to stay later to unload the freight. So, in this example, everyone *lost* money because two components failed to collaborate.

## Malfunctions

In this example, not having the proper attire to enter into the facility is the malfunction. There will be times where it is impossible to know the requirements of what each company requires in order for a driver to pick up or deliver freight; therefore, it is crucial for all parties to collaborate ahead of time. The shipping company should be transparent and communicate the requirements to the broker. If the broker is informed of the requirements from the shipping or receiving companies of what is needed in order to pick up or deliver freight, he or she should verbally tell the driver and document the requirements on the rate confirmation.

## Lesson Learned

Even though all four components work independently, it is necessary for each of them to think of the four components as one team. In order for there to be fewer errors resulting in money being *lost*, each component will need to change its mentality from individual mindedness to teamwork and collaboration. The payoff in making this change will be successful collaboration: each component will stop *losing* money.

In this example, if collaboration is really the focus, the shipping company understands the importance of getting the freight loaded, so they might offer to let the driver use one of their safety vests and hard hats. This is the best solution for this example. By the shipping company offering to collaborate and offer assistance, every component *makes* money by the load being delivered on time. In a situation like this, the driver is equipped with the proper attire and is reminded of the importance of having the proper equipment on his truck and INSIDE of his truck and to be prepared for all situations when receiving and delivering freight. Having the proper attire is just as important in some situations as having the proper equipment on his truck. Collaboration educates, empowers, and problem solves to ensure that the job is done and done well. In an ideal situation, equipment would have been provided or the driver would have been informed of the equipment and attire requirements and all goals would have been met without delay.

Collaboration is the key to keeping the freight moving. If every component truly has the same goal, what is wrong with using a team concept? Having a "big picture" mentality that focuses on team work and collaboration is so important to all components and will ensure that each component is making money and not losing it. Each component needs to be aware of who is willing to collaborate and be more intentional in working with companies that share a similar philosophy of integrity and are willing to work and collaborate with others. Focusing on companies that offer lower rates is not always best. This is where the adage, "You get what you pay for" becomes relevant. When we collaborate with others and focus on providing good, quality service on our own end, we improve all elements of the truck industry and as a result, the value of freight will increase.

## Important Reminders

- Listen and collaborate
- Collaboration is key to building a working relationship
- Lack of collaboration can sever ties and ruin reputations
- Being helpful makes collaboration so much easier for all components
- Use honesty, communication, and knowledge to enhance your collaboration skills
- Think of the four components in the industry as one team trying to achieve the same goal
- Each component needs to focus less on individuality and more on a team concept, enhancing the experience for all
- Don't be hesitate in offering assistance to other components when a need arises; it will pay dividends

- A desire to collaborate should be higher than a desire to focus solely on lower rates
- Collaborate to problem solve, offering solutions to problems that arise on a daily basis. This might mean offering suggestions for reroutes, equipment and attire needs, and malfunctions that occur on a day-today basis for all components

## Chapter 6

# Spy glasses
## (a look inside)

After thinking about the *Top Ten Things About The Trucking Industry That You Don't Know And Why It's Costing You Money*, it's now important to focus on the drivers. You must understand the role of truck drivers. As previously stated, truck drivers are the only component out of the four who deal with each component throughout a single transaction. Truck drivers see what is going on "inside" the shipping and receiving companies and understand what the brokers are trying to do in the industry. Basically, the responsibility of on-time deliveries, undamaged freight and no money *lost* falls on the drivers.

If you think about it, a truck driver can do an awful job of following protocol, arriving on time, and fulfilling his or her obligations but will still get paid. You may decide not to use these types of drivers again in the future but you will always need a truck driver to fulfill your role in the transaction. Understanding the role of a truck driver is very important for all components of the trucking industry and everyone should educate him or herself on this role. With a clear understanding of the world of a truck driver, there is more opportunity for a clear understanding of each component and how, with some collaboration, the processes of these components can work smoothly and efficiently.

There are several types of drivers and jobs in this industry. In order to meet the demands of our country's needs, we *must* continue to support and promote truck drivers through education and knowledge. When looking at statistics and research in this industry, truck drivers are a necessity for our nation to survive. They have an advantage in this industry because they are physically responsible for delivering the service. Shippers, brokers, and receivers are dependent upon truck drivers.

Three major types of drivers, according to ("Wikipedia. 2013" and "*TWNA Glossary - Trucking Terms.* 2001")

- **Owner-Operators:** drivers who own the trucks they drive and can either lease their trucks by contract to a trucking company they are hauling freight for, or they can haul loads for several companies and are self-employed independent contractors
- **Company Drivers:** employees who drive trucks provided by their employer
- **Independent Owner-Operators:** drivers who own their authority; could own a small fleet from 1-10 trucks

Types of truck driving categories:

- Dry Van
- LTL drivers: (Less than truckload)
- Local drivers
- Regional drivers
- Interstate drivers
- Team drivers
- Tanker drivers
- Flat Bed
- Reefer drivers
- Household goods
- Vocational drivers
- Auto haulers
- Boat haulers
- Dry Bulk Pneumatic
- Log Carriers
- Dump Truck

The roles of a truck driver:

- **Pick up freight**: showing up with proper equipment
- **Representative of trucking company**: whether they act professional or rude, drivers are the face of the company
- **Take responsibility of the freight**: understanding the value of the freight
- **Secure the freight, if necessary**: understanding how to secure the freight properly
- **Transport the freight**: safe driving, having knowledge, no damaged freight

- **Directionally gifted**: cannot rely on GPS; need to have an understanding of directions, and map reading skills
- **Common sense**: understanding how to talk to people, being aware of surroundings and knowing the driving laws along the route
- **Great work ethic**: it is important to hire individuals who not only want to work, but know how to work smarter rather than harder
- **Understand the equipment**: understanding the value of the equipment they are using, knowing if they drive fast, it costs more money and can be dangerous, realizing the equipment can cause harm if not operated correctly
- **Understand their skill level**: having self-awareness will allow the driver to know when to take a load or refuse a load
- **Understand time frames**: knowing what time a driver needs to pick up and deliver (Important!)
- **Deliver freight**: making sure it's not damaged and that it does arrive on-time
- **Loading and unloading freight**: drivers need to be aware that this may be required of them (also known as "driver assist")
- **Federal Motor Carrier Safety Administration (FMCSA)**: understanding rules and regulations; keeping up to date with any changes to rules and regulations throughout his or her career in truck driving

There is an extended list of responsibilities that each truck driver is expected to fulfill. People must understand these responsibilities and pressures that each driver faces each and every time he or she places a truck on the road. Arguably, truck drivers are operating the most dangerous vehicle on the road based on the weight of the vehicles they are operating. If an accident occurs involving a tractor-trailer, there is a greater chance people will get injured. Understanding the role of a truck driver will help each component understand the importance of collaboration with drivers; the alternative is choosing to be self-sufficient and exclusive, and potentially setting the transaction up for failure.

How do shipping, brokers, and receiving companies choose the right truck drivers? Is it based solely on who will take the lowest rates? Is it based on reputation of reliability of the trucking company or driver? Remember, you get what you pay for! I feel it will be helpful to understand what drivers actually do so each component can make a more informed decision when choosing a trucking company or driver. Let's take a look at an example how not understanding the role of truck drivers can make you *lose* money.

## Shipping

The shipping company has a hot load that needs to ship as soon as possible. The Logistics Coordinator does not care who hauls the freight; she just wants a lower rate to save money for her budget. She contacts the broker and explains the situation. The Logistics Coordinator and broker were not able to agree on a rate. The Logistics Coordinator contacts a few more brokers. She is upset because all of the brokers refused to accept this load. The brokers are telling the

Logistics Coordinator that because this is a hot load, she must pay higher rates.

The Logistics Coordinator is determined to pay lower rates, so she decides to cut out the broker and find a trucking company to work with directly. Do you think the Logistics Coordinator understands the role of a truck driver? Do you think she understands her high demands should mean paying higher rates? Does the Logistics Coordinator know how to find a reputable carrier since she usually goes through a broker? Logistics Coordinators *must* consider several factors when determining the best decision to ship their freight.

## Brokers

In this example, the brokers understand the role of truck drivers. They understand that in order for them to broker a hot load, the shipping company needs to pay higher rates. The brokers in this example are well informed regarding their company's cost structure along with the price of paying a quality truck driver in order to make a timely delivery on short notice. Due to this understanding, the broker refuses to *lose* money in this situation. The broker could have agreed to a cheap rate, but he could have been stuck with the load or paid a trucking company or owner-operator a higher rate. Either way, the broker would *lose* money.

These brokers did exactly what they should have done in this example. Brokers refusing freight is a bold move in this industry. It needs to happen more frequently in order for the price of freight to be valued. When the price of freight is valued, the expectations for all components will be raised. The industry needs to raise the bar on the standards of quality of service in each component.

## Transporter (Drivers)

In this example, the shipping company has cut out the middle man due to not agreeing on a fair price with the broker. The Logistics Coordinator calls a trucking company to haul the hot load. The same thing happens with the brokers. The trucking company prices the load too high for the shipping company. After making multiple calls to trucking companies and owner-operators, the Logistics Coordinator finally gets an owner-operator to accept her low paying freight.

The truck driver arrives at the shipping company to get the freight. The truck driver enters the facility with a poor attitude and is quite demanding. The shipping employees are displeased with his behavior but need his help to load the freight. The truck driver decides he is not making enough money on this load to help load the freight, so he refuses to help. Remember, this a hot load and needs to be at the receiving company as *soon* as possible. The disgruntled driver sits in the break room, refusing to help load the freight. The attitude of the driver and his refusal to help load the freight are delaying the process of the timely delivery. He does not care. Why do you think he does not care? Maybe he does not understand the time frames. Maybe he does not understand the broker asked him to help load and unload as part of the agreement or maybe his dispatcher failed to communicate this was a "driver assist" load. Whatever the reason, the outcome will not be an on-time delivery. How could this have been prevented? Does the driver understand the importance of his role as a truck driver?

## Receiving

The truck driver is extremely late on the hot load. He provided absolutely no communication en route to the receiving company. The driver took a different route that he thought would save him time. He also stopped and had dinner as he thought he had plenty of time to make the delivery. The receiving company stayed late and paid overtime to their employees because they needed this freight. The receiving company requested that the driver help unload the freight due to its late arrival but once again, the driver refused, excusing himself because he felt the pay he was receiving didn't warrant any extra physical labor on his part. What do you think happened after this situation?

The receiving company is furious and calls the Logistics Coordinator to complain and invoice them for the overtime. The Logistics Coordinator already received complaints from her shipping employees. She also had to pay them overtime since the truck driver refused to help load the freight. So, in the big picture, the Logistics Coordinator failed to understand the worth of truck drivers. By not understanding, she chose to pay a lower rate. This resulted in getting a lower quality carrier, making her company *lose* money.

If you figured up how much extra the shipping company had to pay for the overtime of the employees, it would have justified her paying higher rates for a higher quality trucking company. Instead, her ignorance and lack of understanding *cost* her a great deal of time and money.

## Malfunctions

There will be malfunctions that will result in deliveries not being made on time and this is expected from time to time in this industry. Understanding the role and worth of a truck driver is essential to the growth in all four components, which in turn will result in growth for the trucking industry. Malfunctions sometimes can be prevented with knowledge and preparation. The role of truck drivers in the trucking industry is complex, but their knowledge and skill level can either *deter* malfunctions or *cause* malfunctions. The more you know about a truck driver, the more your component within the trucking industry will be successful.

## Lesson Learned

Truck drivers are a different breed! In general, truck drivers feel special. They have the understanding that just about everything in this world has been delivered by a truck. Think about it: look around in your room, office, public place and you will notice *everything* in that room was hauled on a truck at some point. It is all fascinating! Truck drivers are a necessity for our economy to thrive.

Trucking companies must realize they need to ensure their drivers receive an education on their role in the trucking industry. In this example, when the shipping company needs a truck driver to help unload, it needs to happen without a sense of entitlement or attitude. Drivers are the face of the trucking companies, so making sure they are fostering relationships with every component is imperative to the development of the company or driver in the industry.

In order for all components to work well independently and collaboratively, they *must* understand the role of a truck driver in order to not *lose* money in this industry. The truck driver has the ultimate responsibility of physically making the delivery and doing his or her best to make the delivery on time with no issues, including but not limited to equipment and attire issues, poor attitudes, and demands regarding the transaction at hand. The shipping, receiving, and brokerage companies must make sure they know the qualities they are looking for in a driver or trucking company when it comes to hauling their freight.

## Important Reminders

- Truck drivers are important in the trucking industry
- Truck drivers know what is going on "inside" the trucking industry
- Every component will benefit with a clear understanding the role of a truck driver
- Truck drivers will talk to anyone regarding what is happening in the trucking industry, whether it is positive or negative
- If you want to learn what goes on in the trucking industry, ask to ride with a truck driver
- Truck drivers have a huge responsibility operating one of the most dangerous vehicles on the road based on weight of the vehicle
- Truck drivers have a separate set of rules on the road; knowledge of these rules will help to understand why they may be either frustrated or stressed
- Every component in the trucking industry relies on the driver for the outcome to be achieved

- If a truck driver is being unprofessional or rude, it is a disservice for everyone involved in the transaction
- If a truck driver is ever unprofessional, it needs to be reported to the driver's trucking company and reported to the shipping, brokers, and receiving companies and each component should meet to resolve issues and try to repair the relationship
- Truck drivers are a representative of their company; both negative and positive

## Chapter 7

# Wasting time

Efficiency sounds like another simple concept. In my experience, I have found that many people struggle with efficiency. There is nothing worse than an inefficient person believing they are efficient. I feel efficiency is the only reason I am able to successfully work together with my husband in our company. Efficiency can save you money personally and professionally. Do you know someone in your life who makes multiple trips to the store in one day? Do you know someone in your life who is constantly running errands and looks and acts exhausted? If you take a look at these people in your life and listen to them explain why they are so exhausted, there is a chance they are inefficient.

When running a business, efficiency is money in your pocket. If you or your employees are being inefficient, you are *losing* money. In my personal experience, I have found that when a person is inefficient but fails to admit this inefficiency, resolution is never made. Inefficiency can create a vicious cycle and make a person struggle through each day, attempting to accomplish tasks that need to be completed. It's like a dog chasing its tail. No progress. No order. Only chaos. When you do a snapshot of your day, you should see productivity. The only way to truly reach productivity is through efficiency.

Sometimes in a work setting, an employee will be reprimanded and/or redirected when it is discovered that he or she is being unproductive. There will always be people in your work environment that are not pulling their weight, however, a supervisor must expect accountability in the workplace and require that his or her employees provide proof of the work completed. The best employees are the ones who complete the tasks on their agendas, seek out additional work to help others and make the office run more efficiently, and who want the workplace to be the best it can be. These people are a dream to have on your team!

The goal is to have "efficient-minded" people either working for you or with you. The work load that you will get accomplished will amaze you and not to mention, will make you more money. It is also important to create clearly defined roles for each employee, so there is no redundancy in job tasks. A person must analyze the efficiency level in his or her life. I have created a five step process that will improve inefficiency, allowing an individual to have more time personally and professionally.

**Step 1**: **Identify your level of efficiency**: Sometimes this is difficult for people to do in their lives. I am asking for you to take a snapshot of a day; take a four hour time span and write down everything you did in that time. Once you have your list written down, decide on a scale from 1-10 (1 is the lowest, 10 is the highest) where you would rank yourself. Be honest, only you will see this list and your rating.

**Step 2: Get a calendar**: Make sure you have a calendar; physically writing on a calendar is helpful. If you are someone who uses your phone as a calendar, that works, too. At the beginning of every month, write down every appointment you have in your calendar. If you know of any dates for the upcoming months, please write them down, as well. Once you have your appointments written down, you will not overbook yourself. Also, it is important to not lose your calendar or phone once you write down the important dates. If you are someone who has a tendency to lose items, please get a backup calendar.

**Step 3: Make lists**: I know a lot of people make lists and are still inefficient. I will walk you through a simple way to make and utilize lists. At the beginning of every Monday, you need to make two lists. One list is what you want to accomplish for the week; personally and professionally. On the second list, you need to make a list for Monday of everything you want to accomplish on that day. The tasks that you put on your Monday list should also be on your weekly list. At the end of the day, cross off everything you accomplished on both lists. If you were not able to accomplish everything on your Monday list, ask yourself, "why?" Were you intentional about accomplishing those tasks? After you ponder the efficiency or inefficiency for the day, move on and add the unfinished task or tasks to your Tuesday list. You will make daily lists to assist you in accomplishing your weekly list.

I recommend you make two lists so you don't get overwhelmed. If a person is trying to accomplish tasks on the weekly list, it might feel unobtainable and a person might give up. My weekly list might have 50 tasks to accomplish, but my daily list might only have 10. When you look at a list with 10 items versus 50 items, it makes your day look more hopeful and tasks feel achievable.

**Step 4**: **Analysis**: I like to keep all of the lists that I make and go through them weekly. Sometimes I am not able to accomplish my weekly goals, but by analyzing them I am able to see why I was not able to and consequently make necessary corrections.

**Step 5**: **Weekly, Monthly, Yearly lists**: Once you conquer the task of creating weekly lists and breaking them down into daily tasks, you can move on and create your monthly and yearly lists. These lists are created the same way I showed you on how to create weekly lists. You make a list of what you want to accomplish for the year then break it down by each month. Once the goals are broken down monthly, you can proceed by adding them to your weekly lists.

Efficiency is a choice. You have to be self-aware. Once you analyze there is a problem of inefficiency, you can change your thought process. Trust me, people enjoy being around "efficient-minded" people; especially in the trucking industry. Let's take a look at an example in the trucking industry of how being inefficient can make you *lose* money.

## Shipping

The Logistics Coordinator wants to ship freight by the end of the week. He sends an email to the broker to indicate what he is needing with the load. The broker communicates responds to the email and agrees to broker the load, but requests additional information be provided in order to choose the right trucking company or owner-operator for the job. The broker has difficulty contacting the Logistics Coordinator and after several days and several methods of contact, is unsuccessful. Finally, the Logistics Coordinator calls in a panic asking if the broker has a truck ready to pick up the freight. The broker communicates that she attempted to contact the Logistics Coordinator to request specifics on the load and received no response. As a result, a driver has not been chosen to transport the freight. The Logistics Coordinator apologizes, citing lack of time and organization as the main culprits in this delay of communication. Is it possible this Logistics Coordinator is inefficient? Will this inefficiency ultimately cost his company money?

## Brokers

The broker tells the Logistics Coordinator she can still broker the load, but there is now a time crunch and the load is now considered a hot load. The Logistics Coordinator is in a predicament because the freight *must* be shipped immediately. The lack of planning and communication will make the shipping company *lose* money and the broker is now in a tight spot to find a trucking company or driver to take this hot load. The broker understands that because the load is now considered "hot," she will be forced to pay higher rates. In this scenario, the shipping company and the broker will be *losing* money on this transaction.

## Transporters (Drivers)

The broker contacts several drivers and trucking companies and eventually finds a driver to take the load for a higher rate. The broker has *lost* money on this load due to the inefficiency of the Logistics Coordinator at the shipping company. At this point, the driver is the only one who will be making money on this load.

After the driver drives away to deliver the freight, she realizes she needs to get fuel and catch up her log books. She knows she has plenty of time to make the delivery on time. The driver is also hungry, so she stops to eat dinner along her route. At this point on the trip, it appears the driver will make it to her destination right on time. The unthinkable happens and she gets pulled over for a Department of Transportation (DOT) inspection. What? Doesn't this DOT officer realize the driver *must* make an on-time delivery? Thankfully, her log books are updated and the inspection is successful, however, this delay causes her to arrive to the facility later than scheduled. As a result, the receiving company refuses the load and insists the driver return the following morning. How is this possible? How could the driver have been late when adequate time was given to deliver the freight? Could inefficiency of the driver be to blame for the issues that have arisen?

## Receiving

The receiving company has no choice but to refuse the load based on their company's "no overtime" rule. Again, with the receiving company being the last component to complete the transaction, they find themselves in this predicament often. They are the company that orders the freight and is ensured that it will arrive on time and not damaged. It creates a dilemma that usually results in loss of money. What should they do in these situations? What can they do? This is where inefficiency can make you or another component *lose* money in the trucking industry.

## Malfunctions

Malfunctions will happen in the trucking industry. A lack of efficiency should never be a reason for a malfunction to happen. Inefficiency is man-made; therefore, it can be fixed with self-awareness and a desire to be better for yourself and your company. In this situation, DOT inspections are going to occur and the driver simply did not plan her trip well. She was only planning for the route instead of planning with preparation for the unexpected, which happens daily in the trucking industry. Also, the Logistics Coordinator's poor planning and inefficiency *cost* his company extra money, which in turn *cost* the broker money.

## Lesson Learned

Planning and expecting the unexpected is "par for the course" in the trucking industry. Just when you think the route is smooth sailing, you might experience a blowout, accident, or get inspected by DOT. You never know what is going to happen, so preparation is crucial to being efficient.

A person must identify his or her level of efficiency and adjust accordingly. Once the level of efficiency is identified, it is easier for people to implement procedures to continually improve in this area. Analyzing your accomplishments will empower you to realize what areas you still need to work on in the bigger picture.

There are some people who will never be efficient despite the best of interventions. The "forever inefficient people" must always allow extra time. In this industry, everything happens in a blink of an eye, so efficiency can save a person time, money, and safety. In the example, a lack of planning and a lack of awareness *cost* every component money.

## Important Reminders

- Efficiency is an intentional act that takes practice and persistence
- Inefficiency will not fix itself
- A person must be self-aware and identify his or her level of efficiency
- You must know when you can realistically squeeze in another truck load or not
- Planning is essential to being efficient
- Organization helps create efficiency
- Understanding that the unexpected will occur happen is important to factor into the preparation phase
- Thinking you are efficient when you are not is problematic for you and everyone around you
- People enjoy working with "efficient-minded" people
- Work smarter, not harder
- Those get frustrated when people they are working with are inefficient
- Inefficiency will make you *lose* money
- Make sure you establish clear roles in job duties; redundancy is inefficient
- Being succinct in any type of communication creates efficiency
- Understand your personal worth; know the value of your time

**Chapter 8**

# Broken into pieces

There is a sense of urgency for us when it comes to maintenance. I feel anything that is important to me in my life should receive regular maintenance. This includes both our personal and professional lives. If you are not providing maintenance for what is important in your life, you will experience a breakdown at some point in those areas. If you have a breakdown, it will *cost* you money and possible clientele. If you are not actively providing maintenance on your work equipment and collaborative relationships, you will *lose* money in the trucking industry.

At Ben Freight Trucking, our livelihood is our semi that is driven anywhere from 1800 to 2300 miles per week and because of this, it is extremely important that we regularly maintenance it and make sure it functions the way it was designed to. Just like our semi, we recognize that there are other areas of our lives that need regular maintenance. Relationships need maintenance, too, and this includes business relationships and rapport. What about your house?

Your vehicle? The other day, I noticed that my vehicle was in need of an oil change and regular maintenance. With the daily grind of business, my husband and I have found that it is very difficult for us to personally provide this necessary maintenance for our vehicle. Because of this, we make it a priority and ensure that someone is providing the necessary service the vehicle needs in order to fully function. Unfortunately, our lives do not provide a red light to warn us of much needed maintenance and it is up to us to determine our level of care to be sure that we are functioning to our capacity, as well.

This rolls over to business. Do you realize what should be added to your maintenance list? This is an important step. In order to create your "Priority Maintenance List," you must determine and write down what is most important. You must also recognize that "maintenance" isn't just referring to "fixing your vehicles and making sure they run well." It's not always about spending more and more money. Maintenance includes training, proper attire, taking time to rest, and nurturing relationships in the personal and business worlds. You can follow these guidelines to help you prepare your Priority Maintenance List. Although, personal and professional lists might overlap, it is important to create a "business" and "personal" list to be able to set separate goals for you to see personal and professional results. Once you have created your two separate lists, it will be easier for you to decide where you should focus your attention, time, and money. If you wanted to collaborate with your colleagues, you could share your business list. By sharing your list at work, it can potentially strengthen your partnership and encourage a team concept. Your personal list is for you to monitor your goals on an individual level.

**Guideline 1**: Take a look at your life and write down everything that is of importance to you. Whatever is important to you will require maintenance.

**Guideline 2**: Once you have identified the important areas in your life and work, prioritize them based on the need to have these items maintained. Equipment maintenance in the trucking industry should always be "top priority on the professional list." If not, this will make you *lose* money due to breakdowns, inspection fines, etc.

Another Example: If you have not reached out to a business colleague in several months, you would want to make sure this is on your list. It is important to maintenance business relationships if you want to build solid working relationships.

**Guideline 3**: Implement the maintenance no matter the *cost*. If you wrote it down on the list as being important in your life, maintenance it and you will not regret it. An example: my husband and I were noticing that we were waking up with sore necks and backs so we decided to invest in a new mattress that was expensive but well worth the price. We now notice that we are waking up feeling refreshed from getting rest and because of this, we are much more productive during the day!

**Guideline 4**: Always evaluate your list on a monthly basis. Reflect back on the items you were able to maintenance and take a look at how you feel about the work, time, and money you put into making the important things in your life better. Upon reflection, if you don't feel better or see any benefit after providing maintenance in an area in your life or business, delete that item from your Priority Maintenance List.

These guidelines seem simple to follow but it really is the act of follow through that is important. If you allow important areas in your life to go unkempt, you could experience more chaos, drama, emergencies, and stress. It is always nice to have a plan. I realize a plan cannot always prevent something bad from happening, but at least you will have a plan on how to fix the problem. Being prepared and positive will help minimize the negativity and toxicity that creeps into a person's life and business. Let's take a look at a lack of maintenance in the trucking industry and how it can *cost* you money.

## Shipping

The Logistics Coordinator needs to ship freight out immediately. He is not happy with the current broker the company is using because of the amount of money *lost* on prior transactions. He decides to contact a broker he hasn't worked with in over year. The Logistics Coordinator leaves a voicemail and also sends an email to this particular broker. At the end of the day, the Logistics Coordinator realizes that he has not received a response from the broker so he contacts the headquarters that employs this broker asking to speak with her. The supervisor confirms that the broker is no longer employed there. As a result, the Logistics Coordinator opts to contact the broker who caused such a great loss of money in the past. Apparently, the relationship faded between the former broker and Logistics Coordinator, but why? Who failed to maintenance the relationship? Who does the maintenance fall on in the trucking industry? Does a lack of relationship maintenance make components in the trucking industry *lose* money?

## Brokers

In the example, the broker that has a history of making the shipping company *lose* money, gets the business. Why or how does this happen? As previously mentioned, it can be assumed that the broker and the Logistics Coordinator have failed to maintenance their former positive, working relationship. Even though the Logistics Coordinator chose to use another company because of lower rates, it does not mean they both should have a severed business relationship. Just because a company can provide lower rates does not mean it can provide excellent quality of service. They are not one in the same and sometimes in the trucking industry, this gets misconstrued. And, when the Logistics Coordinator attempted to contact the broker from a former working relationship, why didn't he or the supervisor he spoke with attempt to create a working relationship immediately while communicating on the phone?

## Transporters (Drivers)

The broker finds a trucking company to haul the freight. The trucking company has a great record with on-time deliveries with no damaged freight while working with this broker. This particular trucking company always sends out quality check surveys randomly to ensure their drivers are meeting the demands of the brokers. This company also regularly maintains their equipment.

The driver leaves to make this delivery. On the way to deliver the freight, the driver blows a trailer tire. The blowout was so severe it also damaged the underneath trailer and caused multiple flat tires. How could this happen? Did the truck have proper maintenance? After the repair company fixed the tires, the freight was late and refused until the next morning. This situation seems unfair and unavoidable, so why did everyone *lose* money? The owner of the trucking company knew the tires were worn out, but made the decision to wait to purchase new tires due to the expense of the maintenance.

## Receiving

In this example, the receiving company needs the freight at a specific time to meet the needs of its customers. If freight is not there timely, the receiving company must decline the shipment until the next morning in order for it to work into the schedule. This results in money being *lost* for the shipper, broker, driver, and receiver companies. How can this be prevented?

## Malfunctions

Malfunctions are going to happen in the trucking industry. Some malfunctions are not preventable and some are. In this example, the tires were worn out and needed to be replaced with new ones. As a result of not providing proper maintenance to the equipment, it will now *cost* the company more money due to the extent of the damage incurred. Tires can always blow out while driving; therefore, when you know tires are worn out, it is also best policy to provide maintenance. It can prevent someone from getting hurt or additional damage occurring to the equipment.

## Lesson Learned

When making your list as a business on what needs maintenance, it is a business's obligation to make *safety* a priority. Meeting safety guidelines is always a great start when constructing your Priority Maintenance List. It is always helpful to make sure the equipment is up to date on preventative maintenance and follow through with any additional maintenance on the equipment. Allowing expenses to overshadow the need for maintenance is irresponsible and will end up *costing* you and your company more money in the long run. It will also *cost* other components in the trucking industry.

It is also important to maintain working relationships. Sending any type of communication to continue the relationship is invaluable. Nurturing relationships can be as simple as sending a weekly or monthly email, note of thanks to say thanks for collaborating, newsletter, promotional items with your company's name and logo, or a phone call. When business relationships dissolve for any reason, it is still important to maintain a presence. You never know when a company will be in a crunch and need someone they can trust to handle their business. Maintenance is an easy task that can prevent you and your company from *losing* money.

## Important Reminders

- Maintenance is vital in your professional and personal lives
- Maintenance should include relationships
- Make a list of everything important in your life and realize they all needs maintenance

- If it is important to you, it needs to be maintained
- Maintenance is vital for safety in the trucking industry
- Even though a company dissolves its working relationship with you, maintain the relationship to remain a positive presence in the industry
- Understand when a malfunction is preventable or not preventable; implement a plan for each
- Understand that maintenance needs to happen in all four components in the trucking industry; it does not fall on one specific component
- Take a look at the guidelines in this chapter to ensure you understand what needs maintenance in your life and business
- A lack of maintenance will make you *lose* money and potentially cause you pain

## Chapter 9

# He did what?...She said what?...Who all knows?...

In the trucking industry, word of mouth can help you or it can hurt you. A company has to build a positive reputation in order to be successful and profitable. I have mentioned several reasons why companies are *losing* money in the trucking industry. Whether or not the outcome of each transaction is positive or negative, it will get attention by word of mouth and eventually make it to each component you work with. I personally like "word of mouth" because I know I am running my business with integrity, which results in positive feedback and discussion. So, the more my company is spoken of using words like, "integrity, "honesty," and "efficiency," the happier and more productive I am.

I find it disheartening that it appears that people *expect* dishonesty in the trucking industry. Lies and dishonesty will spread like wildfire by word of mouth. It seems rash to desire to work with a company that bases its value system on a set of lies. Earlier in the book, we determined that it is essential for all components in the trucking industry to shift its paradigm from "one mindedness" to "team mindedness," focusing less on the amount of money earned or saved and more on honesty, collaboration, and teamwork. I believe this shift can happen in the trucking industry. As soon as companies buy into the team concept idea, goals are met, communication is refined, and reputations improve. A natural response to positive feedback with word of mouth is success and prosperity for all.

In trucking, negative feedback through word of mouth is making you *lose* money. If a negative experience happens, the details of the event will spread immediately to many different people, including the ones you work and collaborate with. Companies that do not have quality checks in place to ensure their employees are carrying out the mission and vision of the company are making a big mistake. Doing quality checks will allow you as a business owner to either reward your employees for creating a positive experience for other businesses or allow business owners to create interventions for their employees to improve their deficits.

You want to have a reputable business you can be proud of by completing what you say you will complete. In the trucking industry, if you incorporate the concepts in this book, it will create a trust with customers. Creating trust will turn into a partnership and a long lasting business relationship. Let's take a look at an example to see how word of mouth is making you *lose* money in the trucking industry.

## Shipping

The Logistics Coordinator needs to get a hot load covered immediately. He contacts a broker he heard about through a colleague. The Logistics Coordinator is not satisfied with the rate the broker is making him pay, but he needs this freight shipped, so he agrees to pay the higher rate. Do you think the Logistics Coordinator will tell people he is unhappy about the high rate? Do you think he will discuss his unhappiness with his colleague?

## Brokers

The broker is happy to have the business from the Logistics Coordinator. She also feels great about the rate she was able to squeeze out of the Logistics Coordinator. The broker receives an email from the owner-operator she contacted to ship the freight indicating he will be available to pick up the freight because he will be in the area at the time requested. The broker responds to the email confirming that she will contact him promptly with the rate confirmation. The driver never receives the information regarding the freight. As a result, he contacts the broker by telephone to discuss the specifics, only to find that the broker has chosen not to use his services and instead, found another owner-operator in the area. This infuriates the driver because he cleared his schedule to prepare for the pick-up and now, he has *lost* money as a result. Do you think this broker has been honest with the owner-operator? Do you think the driver is going to share details of this issue with his peers?

## Transporters (Drivers)

The owner-operator who initially wanted the load from the broker felt the broker should have communicated with him regarding the change of plans and hiring of another owner-operator. While corresponding with the broker, the driver had no reason to believe that the broker was being dishonest and would not follow through with the deal. Information was sought and in turn promised that further information would be given. Sadly, this was the not the case and the driver lost out on the deal because the broker did not inform him that another driver had been found.

While sharing the specifics of this situation with a colleague, it was discovered that the broker contacted the colleague to pick up freight. The colleague was the same distance from the pick-up that the driver was, which gives indication that the broker was not willing to be honest with the driver regarding his services. What could have been an honest conversation regarding preference, turned in a lie, causing more issues and trouble for all components involved. Integrity was threatened, money was lost, reputation was marred, and future business was jeopardized. It might have seemed easier to lie about the change in drivers but honesty is much more important here. Too much was lost and recovery could be difficult.

Do you think both owner-operators were happy to find out the broker they use is lying to them? In a matter of hours, word of mouth is creating a reputation for that particular broker and her company. How does this make a company *lose* money? Do you think these two truck drivers will ever trust what this broker tells them in the future?

## Receiving

The owner-operator arrives early to the facility because of a smooth and efficient pick up at the shipping company. The driver is pleased with the early arrival time because it will allow him the opportunity to pick up additional freight from another company before the end of his work day. Much to his surprise, when the driver arrives at the receiving company, the freight is denied by the Supervisor with no explanation provided. The owner-operator is confused and worried from the lack of communication and because he has a pending pick-up with another company. The Supervisor is visibly upset, refuses to explain his reasons for demanding the freight back to its shipping company and refuses to discuss the matter any further. Due to this confusing scenario, the driver is very upset and angrily demands that the Supervisor and his crew unload the freight and deal with the specifics with the shipping company, indicating that he is the driver and should not be penalized for a decision made, in essence, has nothing to do with him. The driver contacts the broker to explain the situation who then requests that the driver take the freight back to the shipping company and as a result, stating that the driver will be compensated for all of this. Regardless of the circumstances that led to the Supervisor to refuse the freight, it seems pretty obvious that he has created some strain in relationship with the shipper, broker, and driver. All three of these components will share their experience with their colleagues in the industry. Word of mouth here can damage the reputation of the receiving company; especially because he was demanding and refused the freight without explanation. Everyone *lost* money in this situation and the receiving company highly damaged its reputation.

## Malfunctions

We have discussed malfunctions and the fact that they will inevitably occur in the trucking industry. People choosing to be dishonest and choosing not to communicate effectively with other components is not a legitimate excuse for a malfunction because it is completely avoidable! In this example, there is a lack of transparency regarding the transaction from the very beginning. The Supervisor at the receiving company could have explained his frustrations and reasoning for refusing the freight to the driver and the broker, and even though the driver had valid reasons for being angry, he could have handled himself more professionally in response to the Supervisor on duty. These outbursts from both parties will make any future correspondence awkward and strained.

## Lesson Learned

Employees in companies serve as marketers of their own company based on their honesty, integrity, and efficiency. Each person has an opinion of the company he or she works for and this opinion can make the company reputable or untrustworthy. How a person feels about his or her position will eventually "leak out" to others via word of mouth. Affirmations will be made evident and complaints or issues with the company will eventually come out and come out at a swifter rate. If a company is well run and functions with a strong value system and with integrity, employees will be pleased and take great pride in the company and refuse to share negatives of the job because they value it so much.

Lies spread quickly; especially in the trucking industry. Truck drivers have a great ear when it comes to gossip from shipping and receiving employees. Brokers need to understand the importance of their role in the trucking industry and learn to be direct and honest, even though they fear it could sever ties with trucking companies or owner-operators.

I guarantee truck drivers are talking to their peers and taking notes on what companies to *use* and which ones to avoid. The goal in this industry is to make deliveries on-time with no damaged freight while making money. I have discussed the importance of moving from one-mindedness and self-sufficiency to a greater team concept in the industry, which will inevitably allow each component to make more money. I feel that integrity is vital to a company's success and should be implemented and introduced as a value in the value system and mission statement of the company. If implementation and follow through takes place, employees, customers, and colleagues will have no reason to spread negative feedback to others. In addition to this, the value system will encourage employees to be honest and forthright about issues regarding integrity, efficiency, and honesty in the workplace. Having a checks and balances can take place between co-workers if done in a respectful and professional manner.

Confronting a peer at work can be awkward and very difficult at times, but if done in a professional manner, it can be less stressful and more beneficial. At first, it is important to be aware that the person acting unprofessionally could be having a bad day or could be dealing with struggles or insecurity, dissatisfaction, defeat or loss. Sometimes, the behavior is a symptom of a deeper issue and should most definitely not be taken personally as it is no reflection of you. Before you confront an unprofessional peer, be aware of *why* you are confronting. Please do not confront just because you want to argue with your peer or because you feel it will help you gain superiority over him or her. The goal in confrontation is to empower, enlighten and to find resolution to the issue at hand. If conflict is handled properly, it can strengthen the relationship. There are several factors to consider when confronting a peer:

1. Be cautious of tone. Make sure your voice is calm. No yelling
2. Be respectful. Use appropriate language. No cursing
3. Understand what must be said to the person and what is not necessary. Degrading someone is not appropriate
4. Do not be defensive
5. Ask the peer you are confronting if there is anything you can help with

## Important Reminders

- Lies spread quickly in the trucking industry
- People do not want to work with dishonest people and will use word of mouth to tell anyone who will listen
- Employees are marketers of their company
- It is a great idea for companies to implement quality checks to ensure their employees are carrying out the company's mission and vision
- Drivers talk frequently to their peers
- Drivers love to hear and spread gossip
- Word of mouth can *help* you as a business but is can also *hurt* you

- Be direct and honest with each other in the trucking industry
- Shift the paradigm from an individual concept to a *team* concept
- Hold each other to a higher standard in the trucking industry and use appropriate confrontation, when necessary

## Chapter 10

# How late are you?...

It might seem absurd to you that a chapter discussing on-time deliveries would be included in this book yet it is another aspect of the trucking industry that is very flawed and continues to cost you and your company money. Delayed deliveries are *costing* all components time, energy, resources, and money and we need to continue the discussion on how to prevent this issue in the future. For the duration of this book, we have discussed the four components of the trucking industry working independently while trying to accomplish the same goal: on-time deliveries with no damaged freight while making money. We have also discussed how this linear thinking and one-mindedness can cause severe problems for the industry and how important it is to work as a team to accomplish our goals. On-time deliveries can only happen when each component completes its role well. There will be times when unforeseen malfunctions occur, resulting in a delayed delivery, but most malfunctions are preventable.

The simple knowledge of why deliveries are not on time is not enough. You can be educated on the reasons these delays occur but until all components work collectively to ensure timely deliveries, things will continue to run as they always have. Prices must be fair, information must be sought and given without delay, people must always practice honesty and integrity, and all of these must work in an efficient manner. Working collectively in a spirit of collaboration will foster greatness in the industry, breaking down the walls of assumptions of how the industry is run, and continue to cultivate positive, professional relationships. This industry is so much more than making money---it's about delivering products that the world needs.

It appears that in most situations, delayed deliveries are caused by preventable malfunctions. With the exception of equipment issues or construction and traffic conditions, there should be no reason for late deliveries. Pertinent information should be acquired, proper attire and equipment should be prepared for and used, routes should be pre-planned (and alternate routes should be provided in case of unforeseen conditions), and communication should always be honest, open, and clear. If these are not completed and a delivery is delayed, trouble-shooting, quality checks, and collaboration should occur immediately to provide accountability and to determine where the glitch occurred. In our industry, it is a default setting to push blame on the drivers but when the quality checks are conducted and research is completed, it is often found that the driver is often set up for failure from the beginning of the transaction by the lack of efficiency and communication with those who set up the transaction as seen time and time again. Let's take a look at an example regarding the importance of on-time deliveries and how a delayed shipment can make you *lose* money.

## Shipping

The Logistics Coordinator receives an order and needs to ship out freight by the end of the week. She decides to seek a broker she has never used in hopes of building a larger list of contacts. In her search for a new broker, she contacts a few of her colleagues to receive feedback on brokers they have used and built positive relationships with. After calling a few brokerages, she chooses a broker she feels encompasses the mission and vision of her own company. The rate is negotiated at a fair price and both parties are satisfied with the agreement. The Logistics Coordinator provides very detailed information regarding the delivery, including freight, time frame, and importance of the freight arriving on time. The freight must arrive at the set time or the receiving company will refuse it. These specifications are very clear. Do you think the Logistics Coordinator feels comfortable with this new brokerage being responsible to haul the freight? Do you think she is worried at all about this broker finding a driver to ensure a timely delivery? These concerns often occur for Logistics Coordinators; especially when depending on others to fulfill their duties in a suitable manner. *Logistics Coordinators have a huge responsibility when going through their selection process to find companies to broker or haul their freight.*

## Brokers

The broker in this example is thrilled to get this freight from a new company. He will do everything he can to safeguard this freight for an on-time delivery. The broker also understands the pressure of getting the job done correctly to ensure that the professional relationship with this Logistics Coordinator continues in a positive manner. This broker has a reputation for being fair regarding pay and is diligent in finding quality truck drivers. The broker finds a trucking company that agrees to haul this freight but the price is much higher than normal rates. As a result, the broker decides to pay the trucking company a higher rate in order to get good, quality work from the driver. With that being said, it is very important to understand that higher rates do not necessarily mean higher quality companies and/or truck drivers.

## Transporters (Drivers)

The trucking company selects a driver with a good reputation who is in close proximity to the location of the freight. Because of a recent decrease in workload, this driver is very happy for the opportunity to haul this freight and after receiving the necessary details from his dispatcher, he rides off to make his delivery. Due to the excitement of the new job, the driver fails to complete his mandatory pre-trip inspection of his equipment.

While en route, the driver finds himself fully absorbed in the conversations of politics that are taking place on the CB. If you have never really been exposed to CB talk, you must know that there is a lot of talking that goes on and it can be very distracting to a driver. This driver finds himself angry and worked up over the political conversation that he becomes distracted from his goal and as a result, misses his exit, taking himself completely off route. Because of his interest in the conversations on the CB and his lack of concentration on the task before him, he has now cost his company extra miles and fuel and has jeopardized an on-time delivery."

In the meantime, the broker contacts the driver to confirm his whereabouts and to inquire on the time of his arrival to the receiving company. In the midst of the confusion from having to re-route, the driver is dishonest and affirms that he will indeed arrive "on time." As the phone conversation ends, the broker asks the driver to contact him when he is nearing the receiving company and the driver agrees to do so. Panic settles in as the driver realizes that this error has cost him a lot of time and as his GPS confirms, he will not arrive to the facility on time. The GPS has re-routed the driver and taken him on a back road to the facility that is forbidden for large trucks. Unfortunately, he is pulled over for this road violation.

After receiving his citation, the driver heads toward the receiving company and while en route, receives a phone call from the broker. The broker is inquiring about the whereabouts of the driver and sadly, the driver lies and tells him that he has reached his destination and that he is preparing to unload the freight. The broker is fooled and the driver pulls into the receiving company an hour later than promised.

## Receiving

The receiving company is bewildered, wondering why the freight has not arrived on-time. The supervisor attempts contact with the Logistics Coordinator and has left several voicemails demanding to know why the freight was delayed. After receiving the messages, the Logistics Coordinator contacts the broker to demand an explanation only to find that the broker is confused because he spoke directly to the driver who indicated that he had arrived at the facility on time.

The receiving company gave very clear instructions and demands regarding the freight, indicating that it HAD to arrive on time or that it would be refused. The Logistics Coordinator agreed to find a broker who would handle the agreement and find a reputable driver to haul the freight. Because the load was not on time, it was refused and sent back to the shipping company. Who *lost* money as a result of the driver not making the delivery on time?"

## Malfunctions

In this example, there are several malfunctions to note: the driver's neglect in checking his equipment and performing his mandatory pre-trip inspection, his concentration on the CB instead of the task at hand, relying on his GPS to re-route him on a safe and legal route, choosing to drive on a forbidden road, and his dishonesty to his broker. This is simply a nightmare for all involved! While it is understood that malfunctions will happen, each and every one of these are inexcusable and irresponsible

## Lesson Learned

This example is a very somber example of a harsh reality regarding the trucking industry. These situations occur often and if there is not close monitoring of trucking companies and drivers, issues will continue to arise and deliveries will continue to be delayed. In this example, each component appears to be competent and willing to work together for a successful transaction.

Truck Drivers must recognize the importance of the tasks they need to accomplish and refuse to be sucked in to the unimportant talk that takes place on the CB. They must focus on completing mandatory inspections and must ensure that the routes are correct and will not lead them in to unlawful situations. They must be honest and forthright regarding their whereabouts and the status of their deliveries. Because the driver chose dishonesty and laziness, all components were affected, and the transaction was unsuccessful.

At the conclusion of this transaction, it is inevitable that details will be shared with other components, resulting in negative backlash for the company and the driver. Marks in reputation are difficult to reverse and it will take time and positive changes to repair the damage.

This example provides a lesson for all components regarding the lack of quality checks in the industry. They simply are not conducted enough and this is why there are so many malfunctions that occur in the trucking industry. Random and scheduled checks are important; especially to prevent complacency and to troubleshoot when a malfunction occurs. It is also important for companies to provide incentives for employees who complete their tasks on time and carry out the mission and vision of the company they represent. If interventions are put into place and executed, the industry is very forgiving and understanding. This is why collaboration and working together is important for us all.

## Important Reminders

- On-time deliveries are the desired outcome in the trucking industry
- If deliveries are not timely, all components will *lose* money
- Paying higher rates does not always mean higher quality trucking companies or higher quality drivers
- In order to make on-time deliveries, there needs to be: communication, honesty, negotiation, efficiency, collaboration, an understanding of the roles of truck drivers, and proper maintenance to equipment and relationships (all have been thoroughly discussed in this book)
- If deliveries are not timely, word of mouth in this industry can destroy a reputation and make restoration difficult
- If deliveries are timely, word of mouth in this industry can help or improve your reputation
- Each component needs to be aware of what is happening inside its own companies
- Create an environment for employees to be honest, communicate ideas and concerns, and collaborate with others
- Create an incentive program for employees; reward employees for working hard and carrying out your company's mission and vision

# Final Thoughts

As I reflect on the content of this book, I am reminded that the trucking industry is considered one of the *most* important industries in our country. I am honored that I work in an industry that is so vital to our nation's existence. Each and every member of each of the components that make up the trucking industry matter. We matter to each other and we matter to the world. When we begin to understand the role of collaboration in our industry and our need for each other, we find that teamwork is essential and provides new perspective, new techniques and strategies, and a solution-focused mindset that delivers. It goes without saying that each component deals with a great deal of stress and trust when it comes to performing tasks in an industry that is often overlooked. Ensuring that you are properly prepared, equipped, and trained in all areas of professionalism will help you navigate through even the most stressful of situations.

My hope is that everything discussed in this book has offered you an opportunity to explore and contemplate and to see things that happen in the trucking industry that are not always clear and transparent. While many of the concepts might seem simple and basic points of business, we have sadly lost sight of them.

At some point, we must abandon all dishonesty, manipulation, and gossip and look to integrity, honest communication, efficiency, and collaboration to represent the trucking industry in a manner that does it justice and gives high regard to those whose drive beside us, load and unload with us, schedule and make telephone calls in the cubicle beside us, and who work diligently to ensure that they are doing the absolute best we can. It is very important to stop focusing on ourselves and shift the paradigm to a team-concept that focuses on all components and empowers them to function successfully. There are no easy fixes, but if we press on toward these values, we are a step closer to being the most sought after, respected industry in the world.

We must not lose sight of the importance of this industry. We must recognize that choosing to refuse to collaborate is a great disservice to our customers who rely on us to deliver their product. We are very important because we aid in the delivery of toys, life-changing medical devices, food, building supplies, government items, vehicles, and many other commodities AND necessities. Be encouraged! The more you work with others to improve the deficits in this industry, the more satisfaction you gain and the more successful your company is. There is nothing more satisfying than working in an industry you believe in. Consider implementing the concepts that have been presented in this book because they matter and *you* matter!

**Top Ten Things About The Trucking Industry**

**Top Ten Things About The Trucking Industry**

## Appendix

# Trucker Talk Defined:

| | |
|---|---|
| **CB:** | commercial band radio |
| **10-4:** | ok, yes |
| **Getting loaded:** | freight being loaded on truck |
| **4 wheeler:** | regular car on the road |
| **18 wheeler:** | semi on the road |
| **Chicken coup:** | roadside scales |
| **Do you got your ears on:** | do you have your CB radio on? |
| **Jet pilot:** | speeding vehicle |
| **Comic books or Swindle sheets:** | log books (daily report of driver activity. |
| **Drop the hammer down:** | pressing the acceleration full speed |
| **Clean and Green:** | no police or obstruction ahead |
| **Checking my eyelids for pinholes:** | i'm tired |
| **Bumper sticker:** | a tailgating vehicle |
| **Bubblegummer:** | teenager in a car on the road |
| **Anklebiters:** | children |
| **99:** | final stop or destination of a load |
| **Disco lights rolling:** | police car with lights on |
| **Bear taking pictures:** | police with radar |

*"Trucker Slang and CB Radio Lingo Dictionary. 2013"*

**Top Ten Things About The Trucking Industry**

## Citation Page

*American Trucking Association.* (2013). Retrieved from
http://www.truckline.com/

Bureau of Labor Statistics, U.S. Department of
Labor, Occupational Outlook Handbook, 2012-13 Edition,
Heavy and Tractor-trailer Truck Drivers,
on the Internet at http://www.bls.gov/ooh/transportation-and-material-moving/heavy-and-tractor-trailer-truck-drivers.htm

*Truckinginfo.com.* (2013). Retrieved from
http://www.truckline.com/

*Trucker Slang and CB Radio Lingo Dictionary.* (2013). Retrieved from http://www.thetruckersreport.com/trucker-slang-and-cb-radio-lingo/

*Twna glossary - trucking terms.* (2001). Retrieved from
http://www.twna.org/trucking_terms.htm

"Wikipedia." *Truck Driver.* N.p., 15 Oct 2013. Web. 21 Oct 2013. <www.wikipedia.org/wiki/truck driver):>.

My hope is that this book has offered insight into real-life scenarios of all components of the trucking industry and how we can all work together to improve the functionality and remove the negative aspects of it. Overall, the industry has offered good experiences for our business but we have also witnessed and spoken to colleagues who have experienced a great deal of dishonesty, manipulation, inefficiency, and great loss of money. With a solid plan of how to proceed in business with honesty, integrity and a value system that positively influences the trucking industry, our days will be filled with less stress, more communication and transparency, and less money lost. Be encouraged that there are others out there who want to work with you and with me to make the trucking industry the best it can be!

I would love to meet with you after reading this book to discuss your thoughts on how we can work together to improve our industry. I would be honored to hear your feedback and suggestions and would love to create opportunities for future collaboration through workshops, seminars, or speaking engagements. When contacting me, please include your name and the best way and time to contact you.

Here's how to find me:

www.truckingsimplified.com, Randi@truckingsimplified.com, www.linkedin.com/in/RandiLParis

P.S. I am looking forward to meeting you and hearing about your business!

## Top Ten Things About The Trucking Industry

Top Ten Things About The Trucking Industry

# About Randi

Randi founded Ben Freight Trucking, Inc. in January 2012 and currently serves as the President and CEO. While attending graduate school at Indiana University-Purdue University-Indianapolis (IUPUI) years ago, Randi lived with her aunt Nancy, a truck driver for over 20 years. Randi recalls the time spent with her aunt very memorable, hearing the fun, crazy trucking stories that her aunt would share. Randi then met her husband, Ben, who was also a truck driver, therefore, the trucking world became a part of her every-day life. After intensively researching the trucking industry, Randi discovered what was missing: lack of honesty, transparency, and communication.

Randi is a Licensed Clinical Social Worker and worked in the social work field for over 12 years. After assisting individuals and families achieves their goals, her passion and focus switched to creating and building a reputable trucking company. With her education, clinical licensure, and work history, she is able to bring a skill set to the trucking industry that is unmatched.

Randi resides in Indianapolis, Indiana with her husband, Ben, her Bichon Frise, Bella, and her Maltese, Lola. She enjoys playing and watching sports, spending time with friends and family, and taking Bella and Lola on bike rides.

For more information visit www.truckingsimplified.com.

**Top Ten Things About The Trucking Industry**

## Top Ten Things About The Trucking Industry

www.ingramcontent.com/pod-product-compliance
Lightning Source LLC
Chambersburg PA
CBHW061449040426
42450CB00007B/1287